ABOUT THE AUTHORS

Ray Leigh is a former editor of the *Billericay Bugle*, columnist on *Darts and Dartmen* and author of such bestsellers as *The Hitchhiker's Guide to Essex*, *A Year in Basildon* and *Bonfire of the VAT Returns*. He lives in a mobile home in Shoeburyness.

Brent Wood is Visiting Lecturer in Linguistics at the University of Ilford and a part-time satellite dish installer. His previous convictions include obtaining money by false pretences and keeping a pit bull terrier without a permit. His best-known published work is *The Ballad of Chelmsford Jail* which was hailed at the time as 'the last word in Essex penal literature'.

D0993390

OTHER JOINT PUBLICATIONS
BY RAY LEIGH & BRENT WOOD

A letter to the *Benfleet Clarion*
protesting at the closure of the
Tellbert Drinking Club.

the
ESSEX
GIRL
joke book

Ray Leigh & Brent Wood

CORGI BOOKS

THE ESSEX GIRL JOKE BOOK
A CORGI BOOK 0 552 13930 0

First publication in Great Britain

PRINTING HISTORY
Corgi edition published 1991
Corgi edition reprinted 1991 (three times)

This book was set in 12/14 Plantin.

Corgi Books are published by Transworld Publishers Ltd, 61–63
Uxbridge Road, Ealing, London W5 5SA, in Australia by Transworld
Publishers (Australia) Pty Ltd, 15–23 Helles Avenue, Moorebank,
NSW 2170, and in New Zealand by Transworld Publishers (NZ)
Ltd, Cnr Moselle and Waipareira Avenues, Henderson, Auckland.

Printed and bound in Great Britain by
Cox & Wyman Ltd, Reading, Berks.

the
ESSEX GIRL
joke book

DEDICATION

To all the girls who made
this book possible

FOREWORD

The tribes of the British Isles are many and various. All contribute much to the rich tapestry of the kingdom.

Essex girls have been with us since Roman times. Perhaps the most famous was Boadicea, the leopardskin-clad warrior queen who cut a swathe through the east of the country in her magnificent chariot, the XRIII, which was custom-built by craftsmen at the ford alongside the hamlet we know today as Dagenham.

But since then, this colourful and fascinating species has been sadly neglected by sociologists. Now, Ray Leigh and Brent Wood have compiled a riveting social documentary, destined to sit alongside *The Ascent of Man* and *Civilisation*.

This *meisterwerk*, drawing on both legend and contemporary reality, faithfully records the language, philosophy and iconography of Essex Girl. I have no hesitation in recommending this work to all serious students of culture and social mores. It is the dog's bollocks.

Professor Theydon Bois
Principal
Romford Library of Video   1991

Why does an Essex Girl wear knickers?

A. To keep her ankles warm.

How does an Essex Girl turn on the light after sex?

A. She opens the car door.

How do you know when an Essex Girl has had an orgasm?

A. She drops her kebab.

What's the similarity between Mikhail Gorbachev and an Essex Girl?

A. They both got screwed on holiday.

What's the difference between Mikhail Gorbachev and an Essex Girl?

A. In Gorbachev's case, there were only eight of them and he knew them all.

What does an Essex Girl say after sex?

A. Do you all play for the same team then?

Why did the Essex Girl wear a leopard-skin leotard?

A. So her dad wouldn't spot her on the back seat of Wayne's Capri.

Why did the Essex Girl go to church?

A. Because she thought she heard they worshipped Rod.

How do you get rid of an Essex Girl?

A. Tell her your car's being repaired.

What's the difference between an Essex Girl and a gerbil?

A. An Essex Girl could never get a date with a Hollywood star

What does an Essex Girl like to wear behind her ears?

A. Her knees.

Why does an Essex Girl take care when she turns off her alarm clock?

A. So she doesn't smudge her make-up.

What's an Essex Girl's favourite TV programme?

A. *Open All Hours*.

What does an Essex Girl do when someone shouts 'There's a mouse in the room!'?

A. She checks her highlights.

What time does an Essex Girl get to work?

A. An hour after she gets home.

Why does an Essex Girl shave her pubic hair once a week?

A. She thinks designer stubble looks attractive on a man's face.

What's an Essex Girl's favourite invitation?

A. Would you like to spend the weekend on my boat?

Why does an Essex Girl wear a bra?

A. Because she likes a little foreplay.

Why didn't the Essex Girl go all the way on her first date?

A. Because the bloke didn't pay for her chips.

Why does an Essex Girl keep her feet out of the bath?

A. She doesn't want her ankle chains to get rusty.

How do you know when an Essex Girl's got her period?

A. She stays in to wash her hair.

What's an Essex Girl's favourite band?

A. Deep Purple.

What's an Essex Man's favourite band?

A. Three Dog Night.

How many Mates does an Essex Girl have?

A. Depends how many packets she bought.

What's an Essex Girl's idea of hard work?

A. Button flies.

How do you know if your secretary's an Essex Girl?

A. There's Tippex on the wordprocessor.

What does an Essex girl call a friend who buys the *Sunday Sport*?

A. An intellectual.

What do you give an Essex Girl after you've been going out with her for two weeks?

A. An eternity ring.

What do you give an Essex Girl before you start going out with her?

A. A full medical.

What's an Essex Girl's least favourite movie?

A. *It Happened One Night*.

What's the difference between an Essex Girl and the TSB?

A. The TSB sometimes says no.

What is an Essex Girl's favourite meal?

A. Meat and two veg.

How does an Essex Girl carry out a pregnancy test?

A. 'You come, Wayne?'

What's the difference between an Essex Girl and the *Titanic*?

A. Fewer people went down on the *Titanic*.

How do you define a 'shy' Essex bride?

A. One who waits until she's been married for two hours before screwing the best man.

How does an Essex Girl like making love?

A. In the mercenary position.

What's the difference between an Essex Girl and Moby Dick?

A. An Essex Girl has swallowed more semen.

What is the Swiss Army Knife Essex Girl attachment used for?

A. Getting feet out of steering wheels.

How does an Essex Girl avoid headaches?

A. Buys a padded dashboard.

Boyfriend asks Essex Girl: 'Why can't we have sex tonight, Stace?'
  'I'm on me menstrual cycle.'
  'That's all right. We can put it in the back of the Capri.'

Why does an Essex Girl wear patent shoes?

A. To check she's still got her knickers on.

How do you find an Essex Girl's G-spot?

A. Promise her a fortnight in Marbella.

Why does an Essex Girl wear cheap perfume?

A. To keep the flies off her kebab.

What does an Essex Girl take before sex?

A. Fourteen large Malibus.

What do most Essex Girls do for a living?

A. Temporary secs.

What's the difference between an Essex Girl and a Cadbury's Cream Egg?

A. It costs 20p to lick out a cream egg.

What is an Essex Girl's favourite Christmas present?

A. Stirrup-shaped earrings.

What is an Essex Girl's favourite wine?

A. 'I wanna 'nother Harvey Wallbanger.'

What is an Essex Girl's favourite book?

A. *The Ann Summers Directory*.

Essex Girl joined a golf club. The professional asked if she'd like a caddy. 'Nah thanks. I've brought me Thermos.'

Then there was the Essex Girl who died in a car crash. They buried her in a Y-shaped coffin.

What did the Essex Girl buy her mum for her birthday?

A. A white patent leather colostomy bag.

Why did the Essex Girl fail her driving test?

A. She forgot to check the mirror before going down on the examiner.

What is an Essex Girl's most essential item of make-up?

A. Clearasil.

Essex Girl at a rugby match. Wayne shouts: 'Great tackle!'
  'Yeah,' says Trace, 'and a neat arse too.'

What's the difference between an Essex Girl and a carpenter?

A. An Essex Girl has longer nails.

What is an Essex Girl's idea of real class?

A. An onyx dildo.

Why does an Essex Girl grow her nails?

A. To get to the really difficult bogeys.

What do Essex Girls like most about policemen?

A. Their shiny helmets.

What's the difference between an Essex Girl's knickers and Alton Towers?

A. You have to pay to get into Alton Towers.

Then there was the Essex Girl who thought Little Red Riding Hood was a novelty condom.

What's the difference between an Essex Girl and a turkey?

A. A turkey doesn't gobble at night.

Why did the Essex Girl wear white at her wedding?

A. Because she kept on the dress she wore for her hen night.

What's an Essex Girl's favourite drink?

A. Seven-Up.

What do you call an Essex Girl with an 'O' Level?

A. Chelmsford Girl.

What do you call an Essex Girl with two 'O' Levels?

A. A liar.

What does an Essex Girl mean when she says she wants to be kissed somewhere warm, wet and smelly?

A. She wants to go to Canvey Island.

Why is an Essex Girl like a washing machine?

A. They both drip when they're fucked.

What's the difference between an Essex Girl and a washing machine?

A. You can dump your load in a washing machine and it won't follow you around for a week.

What's the difference between an Essex Girl and a supermarket trolley?

A. A supermarket trolley has a mind of its own.

Where does an Essex Girl go to meet her friends?

A. The VD clinic.

What makes an Essex Girl's eyes light up?

A. A torch shone in her ear.

What's the difference between an Essex Girl and an ironing board?

A. You can't open the legs of an ironing board.

What's the difference between an Essex Girl and Gary Lineker?

A. Lineker has never scored more than four times in 90 minutes.

What's the motto of an Essex Girl on a Club 18-30 holiday?

A. One swallow doesn't make a summer.

What's the difference between an Essex Girl and a tin of Heinz Tomato Soup?

A. Heinz Tomato Soup contains no artificial colouring.

What's the difference between an Essex Girl and an Essex Boy?

A. An Essex Girl has a higher sperm count.

What is the difference between an Essex Girl and a plate of spaghetti?

A. A plate of spaghetti moves when you eat it.

What's the difference between an Essex Girl and a fish and chip shop?

A. You can't get crabs in a fish and chip shop.

Why did the Essex Girl join an Escort service?

A. Because she always wanted an XR3i.

Where do young Essex Girls do their shopping?

A. Boys R Us.

What's the difference between an Essex Girl's hairdo and a packet of Persil?

A. Persil contains no bleach.

Why don't Essex Girls vote?

A. They can't spell X.

What's the difference between an Essex Girl and Snow-White?

A. Snow-White never slept with more than seven men at once.

What does an Essex Girl say during foreplay?

A. ''Aven't you finished yet?'

Why does an Essex Girl go to a garage?

A. To get a 36,000-mile cervix.

What's an Essex Girl's favourite hymn?

A. O Come All Ye Faithful.

Why do Essex Girls have periods?

A. To give Middlesex Girls a turn.

How did the Essex Girl know it was all over?

A. Her friend said she was on the Wayne.

How do you get ten Essex Girls into a telephone box?

A. Tell them it's a Ferrari Testarossa.

What is an Essex Girl's idea of sophistication?

A. Malibu-flavoured condoms.

Essex Girl says to another: 'Give us a bit of chewing gum, Stace'.
  'I'm not chewing gum, Trace. I've just got a heavy cold'.

Why did the Essex Girl complain about sexual harassment in the office?

A. Because the boss asked her to get down to some hard work.

Why do Essex Girls have blow lamps?

A. To take off their make-up.

Why did the Essex Girl give up aerobics?

A. She couldn't put her legs together.

Why doesn't an Essex Girl snort coke?

A. Because the bubbles get up her nose.

Why did the Essex Girl join Greenpeace?

A. She heard they had a sperm whale.

Then there was the Essex Girl who
thought the Gulf Conflict was a new
Volkswagen convertible.

Essex Girl is asked: 'Is that a Curly Wurly you're eating?'

'Nah, it's a chocolate-covered toffee bar.'

What's the difference between an Essex Girl and an empty crisp packet?

A. You only get one bang out of an empty crisp packet.

Why did the Essex Girl join a golf club?

A. To become the inter-course champion.

What do you call a group of Essex Girls?

A. A Sperm Bank.

What happened to the Essex Girl who bought a vibrator?

A. She knocked all her teeth out.

Why don't Essex Girls go to libraries?

A. Because they can't keep quiet during sex.

Why don't Essex Girls like *Coq au Vin*?

A. They think its cheap to bonk in a Transit.

Where did the Essex Girl go to do her charity work?

A. The Seamen's Mission.

Essex Girl tells her doctor: 'I can only achieve orgasm in the doggy position.'

Doctor replies: 'Don't worry. That's perfectly natural. What's your problem?'

'The dog's got bad breath.'

Then there was the Essex Girl who thought the Renault 21 was a target to aim at.

What's the best chat-up line to use on an Essex Girl?

A. 'The motor's outside'.

What does an Essex Girl say before sex?

A. 'My name's Sharon'.

What's the only word not in an Essex Girl's vocabulary?

A. No.

Then there was the Essex Girl who thought Harvey's Bristol Cream was a massage lotion.

She was the same girl who thought the Common Market was a car boot sale.

She also thought Peter O'Toole was one of the Chippendales.

Why does an Essex Girl ask her man to keep his eyes shut during oral sex?

A. So he can't see her roots.

What's the difference between courting an Essex Girl and a Majorca holiday?

A. There's only a 99% chance of sex on a Majorca holiday.

Why do Essex Girls love snooker?

A. They like men who go in off the pink.

Essex Girl says: 'Wayne, I wanna go to the pictures.'
  Wayne: '*Dick Tracy*?'
  'Only if you buy me an ice-cream.'

What's the difference between an Essex Girl and Margaret Thatcher?

A. No Essex Girl has ever been fucked by men in grey suits.

How do you offend an Essex Girl?

A. Don't know.

What's the difference between an Essex Girl and the complete *Encyclopedia Britannica*?

A. The complete *Encyclopedia Britannica* is impossible to pick up.

An Essex Girl was asked what she thought about the Green Belt.

She said you shouldn't wear it with a pink frock.

How do you make an Essex Girl laugh on a Sunday?

A. Tell her a joke on Friday.

How does an Essex Boy tell an Essex Girl he wants her to be the mother of his children?

A. 'Shit, the johnny's split.'

How does an Essex Girl get dinner for her guests?

A. 'Hello, is that Pizza-to-Go?'

Why do Essex Girls eat vegetables?

A. To increase their IQs.

What's the similarity between an Essex Girl and Lionel Richie?

A. They're both easy like Sunday morning.

What's the difference between an Essex Girl and Lionel Richie?

A. Lionel Richie doesn't bleach his moustache.

Boyfriend asks Essex Girl: 'Fancy trying something from the *Kama Sutra*?'
  'Nah, I don't like Indian food.'

What's the difference between an Essex Girl's private parts and a tube of glue?

A. You might consider sniffing a tube of glue.

What's an Essex Girl's mating cry?

A. 'I'm soooooo drunk.'

Why do Essex Girls smoke?

A. To make their mouths smell like ashtrays.

Why do Essex Girls feel an affinity with Dagenham men?

A. Because they both spend a lot of time in Fords.

What's the similarity between an Essex Girl and Oliver Twist?

A. They both asked a man for more.

What's the difference between an Essex Girl and Oliver Twist?

A. He eventually found out who his father was.

What's the difference between an Essex Girl and Arsenal FC?

A. Arsenal have never gone down.

Why does an Essex Girl hate Father Christmas?

A. Because he comes only once a year.

Why did the Essex Girl buy the *Sunday Sport*?

A. She wanted to impress her friends.

Then there was the Essex Girl who went to Paris and asked what the French was for *soixante-neuf*.

What do Essex Girls eat to increase their bust size?

A. Silicone chips.

Why did the Essex Girl go to work at a leather factory?

A. She wanted to get a quick tan.

What's the difference between an Essex Girl and Mount Everest?

A. Only a few people have been up Mount Everest.

What's the difference between getting piles and breaking off an engagement to an Essex Girl?

A. When the piles clear up you get your ring back.

What's the difference between courting an Essex Girl and travelling on the Starship Enterprise?

A. The Starship Enterprise only goes where no man has gone before.

What is an Essex Girl's favourite French novel?

A. *The Hatchback of Notre Dame.*

What birthday present do you buy an Essex Girl who's been studying Zen philosophy?

A. A vibrator.

What's the difference between an Essex Girl and a carpenter?

A. An Essex Girl's handled more tools.

What's the difference between an Essex Girl and a Lotus Elan?

A. A Lotus Elan's more difficult to get into.

What's the difference between an Essex Girl and hand-me-down clothes?

A. You know who's been inside hand-me-down clothes before.

What's the difference between an Essex Girl and a mirror?

A. You can't see through a mirror.

What's the difference between an Essex Girl and a condom?

A. You only use a condom once.

What's the difference between an Essex Girl and a toffee apple?

A. A toffee apple is more difficult to eat.

What's the difference between an Essex Girl and the *Reader' Digest* subscription department?

A. You can eventually say no to the *Reader's Digest* subscription department.

What's the difference between an Essex Girl and Russian roulette?

A. With Russian roulette you've only got a one in six chance of getting fucked.

What's the difference between Essex and Mars?

A. There might be intelligent life on Mars.

What's the similarity between an Essex Girl and a vampire?

A. They both bite your neck at night.

What's the difference between an Essex Girl and a vampire?

A. Garlic is enough to put a vampire off.

Why is there a university in Essex?

A. So that Kent girls can study away from home.

What's the difference between an Essex Girl and a bottle of paracetamol?

A. It's harder to get into a bottle of paracetamol.

What do you get for screwing ten Essex Girls?

A. A gold medallion.

What is an Essex Girl's favourite cigarette?

A. More.

What's the difference between an Essex Girl's teeth and Billy Bonds?

A. Billy Bonds was only capped once.

Essex boy going down on Essex Girl.
  'What a big pussy. What a big pussy.'
  'There's no need to say it twice, Wayne.'
  'I didn't. That was the echo.'

What's the difference between an Essex Girl and children fighting in a playground?

A. It only takes children a few minutes to make up.

What's the difference between Essex Girls and Hell's Angels?

A. Hell's Angels wear originals.

What's the similarity between an Essex Girl and an electric light ?

A. You can turn both on with the flick of a finger.

What's the difference between an Essex Girl and a 20-watt light bulb?

A. A 20-watt light bulb's brighter.

What's the difference between an Essex Girl and a Jeffrey Archer novel?

A. A Jeffrey Archer novel is harder to penetrate.

What's the difference between Crufts and a Romford nightclub?

A. There aren't so many dogs at Crufts.

One Essex Girl says to the other: 'What do you reckon to Harry Connick Junior?'
  'I don't know nuffink about primary schools.'

What's the difference between an Essex Girl and Sir Ralph Halpern?

A. Sir Ralph only did it five times a night.

Then there was the Essex Girl who thought Berni Inn was a sexual request.

What's the difference beween an Essex Girl and a Kit Kat?

A. You only get four fingers in a Kit Kat.

Why do Essex Girls get married?

A. So they can appear in *Readers' Wives*.

What's the difference between an Essex Girl and a pine table?

A. It's more difficult to strip a pine table.

Why do Essex Girls dance round their handbags?

A. Have you ever met any Essex boys?

Essex Girl looks in a mirror and says to her friend: 'Oi, Trace, do you think I'm getting crow's feet.'
  'Might be. But keep your shoes on and no-one will notice.'

What do you say to an Essex Girl who's too young for sex?

A. 'Coochie coochie coo.'

What's an Essex Girl's idea of an obstacle course?

A. Shell suit trousers.

What's the difference between courting an Essex Girl and fishing in the River Thames?

A. You're less likely to catch something nasty in the Thames.

How do you confuse an Essex Girl?

A. Take her out in a left-hand-drive car.

Why do Essex Girls only eat a third of their Mars Bars?

A. Who needs to work or rest?

How does an Essex Girl tell who she's having sex with?

A. She holds her cigarette up to their face.

What's the difference between an Essex Girl and a walrus?

A. One's got a moustache and smells of fish and the other one's a walrus.

Why doesn't an Essex Girl say very much on a first date?

A. She doesn't like to talk with her mouth full.

Wayne says to Essex girlfriend: 'Why do your feet move up and down when we make love?'

'Cos you keep forgetting to pull me tights down.'

What does an Essex Girl do to men who gatecrash her party?

A. Throws them out in the morning.

How does an Essex Girl change a lightbulb?

A. 'Wayne, get over here...'

What does an Essex Girl call a girl who has ten blokes in one night?

A. Lucky.

What's the difference between an Essex Girl and a hospital patient?

A. An Essex Girl doesn't say 'ah' before she opens her mouth.

What's an Essex Girl's favourite book?

A. Don't be stupid.

What's the difference between an Essex Girl and the man from Del Monte?

A. The man from Del Monte sometimes says No.

Why did the Essex Girl join AA Relay?

A. So she always knows a man who can.

Why did the Essex Girl enter the tennis tournament?

A. She thought the mixed doubles was a cocktail-drinking contest.

How do you find an Essex Girl's clitoris?

A. Turn left at the handbrake.

How does an Essex girl get rid of unwanted pubic hair?

A. Spits it out.

What do you call an Essex Girl who has sex in a Mark III Ford Cortina?

A. A traditionalist.

Why doesn't an Essex Girl ever panic?

A. Because she takes everything in her stride.

How does an Essex Girl know when her bloke is serious?

A. When he puts her name on his windscreen.

What's the difference between an Essex Girl and the doggie on the back shelf of a car?

A. The dog doesn't nod its head as much.

What's the difference between an Essex Girl and Radio Five?

A. You can't pick up Radio Five in a car after dark.

Why did the Essex Girl let her hair down?

A. Because Wayne came in her bun.

What does a poor Essex Girl use for protection during sex?

A. A bus shelter.

What's the difference between an Essex Girl and a food blender?

A. You've got more chance of getting your dick out of a food blender.

Did you hear about the Essex Girl who became an Avon Lady?

A. Max Factor.

Why do Essex Girls dye their hair blonde?

A. Because they want to look more intelligent.

Why did the blonde Essex Girl dye her roots black?

A. Because she didn't want to look out of place.

Why did the Essex Girl stand for Parliament?

A. Because she heard the House of Commons had 650 members.

Why is an Essex Girl like a man in a dirty raincoat?

A. They both like *Men Only*.

How does an Essex Girl tell the difference between margarine and butter?

A. She asks someone to read the packet for her.

What's the difference between an Essex Girl and a Chinese meal?

A. You want another Chinese meal an hour later.

What's the difference between an Essex Girl and Directory Enquiries?

A. You can sometimes get through to Directory Enquiries.

Why is an Essex Girl like a cinema-foyer hot dog?

A. You wouldn't want your friends to catch you eating one.

What do you call an Essex Girl with brown hair?

A. A disgrace to her county.

Why do Essex Girls wear blouses with shoulder pads?

A. So that their men have somewhere comfortable to rest their knees.

What do you get if you cross an Essex Girl with a computer?

A. A system that will always go down on you.

Why does an Essex Girl shave her armpits?

A. To stop her sticking to the Velcro fastenings in Wayne's shell suit.

What is an Essex Girl's idea of a really classy meal?

A. A wooden chip-fork with her takeaway.

Why does an Essex Girl paint her nails?

A. So she doesn't break them getting the last bit of meat off her Kentucky Fried Chicken.

Why is an Essex Girl like a pint of John Bull bitter?

A. They both get drunk in Romford.

What's the difference between an Essex Girl and the Marx Brothers?

A. An Essex Girl wouldn't dream of spending a night at the opera.

What's the difference between an Essex Girl's teeth and Spud U Like?

A. Spud U Like has fewer fillings.

What do Essex Girls do for the environment?

A. Buy unleaded eyebrow pencils.

What's the difference between an Essex Girl's tights and a window cleaner?

A. A window cleaner has fewer ladders.

Why do Essex Girls tell Essex Girl jokes to one another?

A. They're the only jokes they can remember.

Essex Girl and her boyfriend are making love in the back of a car without any protection.

'Oi, Wayne, do you want me to have a baby?'

'Oh yes, Trace, oh yes. If it's a boy I want him to be a boy scout, just like wot I used to be.'

'Well if you leave it in there, it'll be a brownie.'

What's the difference between an Essex Girl's boobs and a week-old bunch of flowers?

A. One droops and smells disgusting. The flowers aren't too good either.

Why do Essex Girls always lose at chess?

A. They can't get over the fact that there isn't any cocktail sauce for the pawns.

Essex Girl complains that her boyfriend has only got a small organ.

Wayne replies: 'Well it's never had to play in a cathedral before'.

Why do Essex Girls always lose at Monopoly?

A. They're always waiting to be picked up at Liverpool Street station.

Why do Essex Girls have onions in their doner kebabs?

A. To make their breath smell sweeter.

Why is an Essex Girl like a West Ham supporter?

A. Because they're both forever blowing bubbles.

What's the difference between an Essex Girl and the England cricket team's bowling?

A. Most men wouldn't catch anything off the England cricket team's bowling.

What's an Essex Girl's idea of romance?

A. A lift home afterwards.

Why do Essex Girls hunt in pairs?

A. So they have someone to keep score.

Why is an Essex Boy like one of the Johnny Mann Singers?

A. Because they're both Up Up and Away.

What does an Essex Girl think of Basque Separatists?

A. She prefers teddies.

What's the difference between an Essex Girl and a hungry Labrador whose owner has just died?

A. An Essex Girl whines more.

Why don't Essex Girls wear lipsalve?

A. They don't mind getting a chap on their lips.

What's the difference between an Essex Girl and a jumbo jet?

A. A jumbo jet's only got one cockpit.

What's an Essex Girl's nightmare holiday?

A. Two weeks on the island of Lesbos.

Why does an Essex Girl have C&A stitched into her knickers?

A. So she knows which way round to put them back on.

Essex Girl to her friend: 'Do you like Chanel No 5?'
   'Nah. I only watch Sky One.'

Why do Essex Girls wear earrings?

A. Because they want to look like their fathers.

'What's the matter with you?' the Essex Girl asked her mum.

'I'm going through the change.'

'Well if you find any 50p pieces, give them to me. They come in handy for the condom machine.'

What does an Essex Girl hope to buy at a Tupperware party?

A. A vibrator.

How does an Essex Girl get a lift home?

A. 'I've never had it in a Sierra.'

What's the difference between an Essex Girl and the Grand Old Duke of York?

A. The Grand Old Duke of York only had 10,000 men.

What do you call twenty-four Essex Girls floating down the Thames?

A. The Isle of Dogs.

What's an Essex Girl's favourite kind of date?

A. Eat Me.

What's an Essex Girl's favourite convenience food?

A. Fish fingers.

What does an Essex Girl do with her arsehole after sex?

A. Asks him to drive her home.

What's the similarity between an Essex Girl and a cowpat?

A. They get easier to pick up with age.

What's the difference between an Essex Girl and an Alsatian?

A. Lip gloss.

Why does an Essex Girl like a car with an adjustable steering wheel?

A. More headroom.

What's the difference between an Essex Girl and a fridge?

A. A fridge doesn't fart when you take your meat out of it.

What does an Essex Girl have written on the back of her knickers?

A. Next.

What's the difference between an Essex Girl and Sooty?

A. You can only get one hand up Sooty.

What's the similarity between an Essex Girl and a carpenter?

A. They've both got a box full of saws.

Why does an Essex Girl wear a fur-trimmed nightgown?

A. To keep her ears warm.

And finally, just to show that Essex Girls aren't the only ones who are good for a laugh...

What does a *Surrey* Girl do the day after a gang bang?

A. Writes twenty thank-you letters.